THE B IRISH LIMERICKS

By
Myler MaGrath

The Limerick packs laughs anatomical
Into space that is quite economical
    But the good ones I've seen
    So seldom are clean
And the clean ones so seldom are comical.

MERCIER PRESS

MERCIER PRESS
P.O. Box 5, 5 French Church St., Cork
16 Hume St., Dublin 2

© Myler Magrath, 1985
Reprinted 1986, 1991, 1992, 1993, 1995
British Library Cataloguing in Publication Data

Magrath, Myler
    The book of Irish Limericks.
    1. Limericks
    I. Title
    821'.07   PN6231.L5

Printed in Ireland by ColourBooks Ltd.

'Far dearer to me than my Treasure'
An Irish lassie said, 'is my leisure,
       For then I can screw,
       Each rich yachtman's crew
They're slow but it lengthens the pleasure.'

* * *

There once was a boring Irish priest,
Whose sermons one felt never ceased.
       His hearers, en masse
       Got fatigued to the ass,
And slept through the most sacred Feast.

* * *

An Englishman near Dublin Bay,
Was Cuckolded by night and by day.
       He murmured, 'Dear, dear,
       I should interfere,
But I feel I'd be just in the way.'

* * *

There once was a lassie from Bandon,
Who said to her man : 'Keep your hand on,
       I admire your technique
       It's simply unique
But my breasts are to love — not to land on.'

* * *

A lassie from this side of Rathmore,
Was wed to one hell of a bore,
    A dopey old farmer,
    To lazy to warm her,
All he did every night was just snore.

*   *   *

There was a young lassie from Crosser,
Who in spiritual things was a messer.
    When sent to the priest,
    This lewd little beast,
Did her best to seduce her confessor.

*   *   *

A young Irish farmer named Willy,
Whose behaviour was frequently silly,
    At a big farmers' ball,
    Dressed in nothing at all,
He claimed he came there as a filly.

*   *   *

The Irishman said with a grouch,
'Tis Winter when you sneeze and you slouch,
    You can't take your women,
    In a canoe or swimming,
But a lot can be done on a couch!'

*   *   *

A young Irish lassie named Smith,
Whose virtue was largely a myth:
  'Try hard as I can
  I can't find a man,
Whom it's fun to be virtuous with.'

   * * *

A young Irish lad like a giant
Who in sexual ways was just quaint,
  One day he went swimming
  With twelve naked women,
And deserted them all for a pint.

   * * *

Two tourists at fair Salthill Strand
Who tried to make love on the sand.
  The Garda on duty
  Said : 'No, me proud beauties
Them foreign contortions is banned.'

   * * *

A 'Rose of Tralee' with such graces
That her curves cried aloud for embraces
  'You look,' cried each he
  'Like a million to me,
Invested in all the right places.'

   * * *

There was a young lass from Listowel
Whose beauty was everyone's goal
    In her efforts to please
    Spread a well known disease,
From Slea Head to the frosty South Pole.

*   *   *

A priest who got up with the dawn,
Saw a lass near a bush in Gougane,
    'Excuse me, dear Miss,
    It's sinful to piss,
On the sacred and blessed green lawn.'

*   *   *

A lassie at Cahermee Fair,
Was having her first love affair.
    As she climbed into bed
    To the tinker she said :
'Do you mind if I start with a prayer ?'

*   *   *

There was a young lass from Rosscarbery,
Who started to count every calorie.
    Said her boss in disgust :
    'If you lose half your bust —
Then you're worth only half of your salary.'

*   *   *

A young lass on a yacht in Glandore,
So tired she could do it no more,
    'But I'm willing to try
    So where shall I lie ?
On the deck, on the sail, or the floor ?'

*   *   *

To an Irishman landing in Heaven
Said St Peter : 'We dine sharp at seven
    Then breakfast's at eight
    Never mind if you're late
And there's Irish crubeens at eleven.'

*   *   *

Said the sharp-eyed Irish detective
'Can it be that my eyesight's defective ?
    Has your east tit the least bit
    The best of the west tit ?
Or is it a trick of perspective ?'

*   *   *

A young lad from near South Donegal
Who went to a Fancy Dress Ball
    Dressed up like a tree
    But he failed to foresee
His abuse by the dogs near the hall.

*   *   *

A lass from the wild Maharees
Was weighed down by B.A.'s and B.D.'s
        She collapsed from the strain
        Alas it was plain
She was killing herself by degrees.

*　*　*

There was a young lady near Glin
Who was strong on Original Sin.
        The priest said : 'Do be good,'
        She said : 'I would if I could.'
And started all over again.

*　*　*

There was a young blade from near Youghal.
Who found he had only one ball,
        Obsessed by his wants,
        He discarded his pants.
In his kilts he is now loved by all.

*　*　*

A lass on the road to Goleen,
Met a baker with a drop of poteen,
        Five minutes of lovin'
        Put a bun in her oven,
The next time she won't be so keen.

*　*　*

A homo who lived in Macroom,
Took a lesbian up to his room,
    And they argued all night
    As to who had the right,
To do what, and with which, and to whom !

*   *   *

A young lass from near Buttevant,
Who said that she knew what it meant —
    When he asked her to dine,
    Private room, lots of wine —
She knew, oh, she knew, but she went.

*   *   *

In Waterford lived a fair lass
Who always wore panties of brass
    When asked : 'Don't they chafe.'
    She said : 'Yes. But I'm safe
From pinches, and pins in the grass.'

*   *   *

A buxom young tourist near Roscrea
Who hung by her toes in a doorway
    She said to her man
    'Just look at me, Dan
I think I've discovered one more way.'

*   *   *

There was an old monk from Kilcrea,
Who of fasting grew tired every day.
    Till at length with a yell,
    He burst from his cell.
'From now on I'm going to be gay.'

      *   *   *

There was a young lass from near Midleton
Who had such a very short skirt on.
    That the curate said : 'Dear,
    You look very queer,
Have you really a skirt or a shirt on ?'

      *   *   *

There was a young man near Dunowen,
Who strolled by himself all alone.
    He's a face like a hatchet,
    I defy you to match it,
Said he : 'I don't mind, it's my own.'

      *   *   *

An old maid from near Castlegregory
Whose morals turned out just a mockery
    For under her bed
    Was a farmer, instead
Of the usual bit of old crockery.

      *   *   *

A woman from outside Killarney
Suspected her son was a fairy,
'It's quite odd,' said she,
'That he sits down to pee,
And he stands just to make me contrary.'

* * * * *

A woman from near Templenoe
Her husband was awfully slow
They kept at it all night,
And got everything right,
For practice makes pregnant, you know !

* * * * *

A lassie from Borriskane
Who went and undressed in a train,
A saucy old porter,
Saw more than he ought-er,
And asked her to do it again !

* * * * *

In Ireland a young guard on the beat,
Saw a couple more fond than discreet.
'Though a Miss, miss a kiss,
Give the next kiss a miss —
For a kiss is amiss in the street.'

* * * * *

A Seanacaidhe back from Dunquin
He married three wives for a whim.
  When asked : 'Why the third ?'
  He said : 'One's just absurd
And bigamy, lads, is a sin.'

* * *

A farmer from near Castlemaine
He courted a girl all in vain
  She fumed when he kissed her
  So, he slept with her sister
Again, and again, and again.

* * *

A man from the wild Blasket Isles
Who suffered severely from piles
  He couldn't sit down
  For fear he would drown
So he had to row standing for miles

* * *

A farmer from Newcastlewest,
Who courted a maiden with zest.
  So hard did he press her,
  To make her say, 'Yes, sir,'
That he broke the ould watch in his vest.

* * *

There was a young man from West Cork,
Whose Da made a fortune in pork.
    Last Sunday at three,
    He was married to me —
Because we're expecting the Stork !

*   *   *

There was an old man from near Croom,
Who kept a baboon in his room.
    'It reminds me,' he said,
    'Of a friend who is dead,'
But he never would tell us of whom.

*   *   *

A young lass from far Limerick South
Who came back from a trip to Bournemouth
    Her father said : 'Nelly,
    There's more in your belly,
Than ever went into by mouth.'

*   *   *

A lass from near Caheracutter,
Who fancied herself in a sweater
    Three reasons she had
    To keep warm was not bad,
But the other two reasons were better.

*   *   *

In Carlow a pretty young lass
Had a truly magnificent ass.
    Not rounded and pink
    As you possibly think.
It was brown, had long ears and ate grass !

       *   *   *

A tourist in Kerry named Jones
Who reduced many Roses to moans,
    By his wonderful knowledge
    Found out while in College,
Of womens' most ticklesome zones.

       *   *   *

A lass on the banks on the Bride,
Whispered love to the man at her side.
    'I never could quite,
    Believe till tonight,
Our anatomies would coincide.'

       *   *   *

The thoughts of the rabbits on sex,
Are seldom if ever complex.
    For up on Cape Clear
    They make love without fear,
And do just as a Gaelgoir expects.

       *   *   *

There was a young lady from Cork,
Whose Da made a fortune in pork !
    He got for his daughter
    A Derry husband who taught her —
To balance green peas on her fork !

*   *   *

On Kathleen's white bosom there leaned
The jaw of a wild Irish fiend.
    But she pulled up his head
    And sarcastically said :
'Mo Bhuchail, won't you ever be weaned ?'

*   *   *

God's plan made a hopeful beginning,
But Irishmen damned it by sinning.
    We hope that the story
    May end in God's glory.
But at present the Irishmen's winning !

*   *   *

There once was an old Irish priest,
Who lived almost fully on yeast,
    For, he said : 'It is plain
    We must all rise again,
And I want to get started at least.'

*   *   *

There once was a man from Glanmire,
Who was seized with a carnal desire.
  And the primary cause,
  Was an ould woman's drawers,
Hung up for to dry by the fire !

* * *

Said a missioner in old Ballycotton,
'The waltz of the devil's begotten !'
  Said Jones to Miss Joy
  'Never mind the ould guy,
To the pure almost everything's rotten !'

* * *

A young lassie from sweet Ballybunion
Whose kisses were sweeter than honey
  The Irishman galore
  Would line up at her door
All willing to pay her some money.

* * *

There was a young lass from near Corrymeala
Who went to a dance as a dahlia.
  When the petals unfurled
  Twas revealed to the world
That the dress as a dress was a failure.

* * *

A flashy young tourist at Brandon,
Whose feet were too narrow to stand on.
    So, she stood on her head —
    'For my motto,' she said.
Has always been — *Nil desperandum !*

*   *   *

A fat tourist from near Ballyheigue,
Whose shoelaces once came untied.
    She feared that to bend
    Would display her rear end —
So, she cried and she cried and she cried.

*   *   *

In Ballybunion some visitors will go
To see what no person should know.
    But then there are tourists,
    The purest of purists —
Who say 'tis uncommonly low !

*   *   *

Concerning the bees and the flowers,
And the birds singing near Slievenagower.
    You will spot at a glance
    That their ways of romance
Don't look one bloody bit like do ours !

*   *   *

A young lad from outside Dunleary
Of girls was exceedingly wary,
    Till a tourist named Lou.
    Show him how and with who,
He could make the long evenings more cheery !

*   *   *

An Irish virgin antique
Locked a man in her house for a week.
    He entered her door
    With a shout and a roar,
When he left he barely could squeak !

*   *   *

A lass a few miles from Ardfert,
Used to jog 'till her corns did hurt,
    But now she just stands
    In the square on her hands
With her head covered up by her skirt.

*   *   *

A woman from sweet Donegal
Had triplets almost each Fall.
    She was asked how and wherefore
    Said : 'Sure that's what we're here for,
But betimes we got nothing at all.'

*   *   *

There once was a man from near Clonmel
Who said : 'They can all go to hell
    What they do to my wife,
    Is the curse of my life —
And, God blast them, they do it so well !

*   *   *

A student who came from Kanturk,
And was rather too frequently drunk,
    Said : 'Sometimes I think
    That I can parse pink,
Let me see : It's pink, pank and punk!'

*   *   *

A lassie from near Carbery's Isle,
Had the ugliest bottom for miles.
    But a blacksmith took pity
    And made it quite pretty,
All dimples, and poutings and smiles !

*   *   *

A comely young woman from Bandon,
Was ravished three times in a landau,
    When she cried out for more,
    Came a voice from the floor —
'The name Miss is Simpson, not Sandau.'

*   *   *

A tourist at Mullaghanattin,
Was fond of a bit of hard petting.
     She claimed to be chaste
     And it seemed a great waste,
But her statement I'd say needs some checking.

*   *   *

A young Irish lass once said — 'Why
Can't I look in my ear with my eye ?
     If I put my mind to it,
     I'm sure I can do it.
You never can tell till you try.'

*   *   *

There was a young tourist in Eskine,
Whose looks admiration did win.
     When I said to her : 'Grace,
     You'd look nice in lace.'
Said : 'In fact, I look best in my skin.'

*   *   *

A farmer from near to Croagh Patrick
Who strangled his wife with a halter.
     Said he : 'I won't bury her —
     She'll do for the terrier
So, I'll hide her, and clean her, and salt her.'

*   *   *

In Belfast dwelt a sweet maid,
Who swore that she wasn't afraid,
  But a farmer from Derry
  Came after her cherry —
'Twasn't just an   advance — 'twas a raid !

    * * *

In Waterford town on the dole,
At last I have reached my life's goal.
  With a hundred a week
  No. T.D. has the cheek —
To ask me to work, Bless their soul !

    * * *

In the ancient old town of Kinsale,
Where there's lashin's of beer and of ale,
  Where each man despite strife,
  Lives with his own wife.
If you've heard something else — it's a tale !

    * * *

Near the Barracks there lives a young lass,
Who is said to have two breasts of brass.
  A soldier who bit her,
  Found in one a transmitter,
For she works for the news house of Tass !

    * * *

Sure, I dine at the best spot in Cork,
On the best of pig's head and of pork,
I eat spuds and boiled eggs,
And turkey-cocks legs,
And I don't have to use knife or fork !

* * *

A lass near the bay of Blacksod
Thought babies were made up by God !
But 'twas not the Almighty
Who pulled up her nightie,
'Twas a clot from Valentia, by God.

* * *

A man from near Galway Station,
Who was found by a pious relation,
Making love in a ditch
To — I won't say a bitch —
But a girl who had no reputation.

* * *

A lassie from Liscannor Bay,
Was asked to make love in the hay.
She jumped at the chance,
But held on to her pants.
For she never had tried it that way !

* * *

An Irishman lay in a hearse
And said : 'Sure, and this could be worse.
    Of course the expense
    Is simply immense,
But it doesn't come out of my purse !'

*   *   *

At a Fancy Dress Dance in Tahilla,
A tourist went there as a pillow,
    When the feathers fell out
    It revealed to the crowd,
That as clothing the dress was a killer.

*   *   *

There once was a lass from Banteer,
So enormously large that, oh dear —
    Once far out in the ocean
    She made such a commotion,
That the Russians torpedoed her rear.

*   *   *

A farmer from near Skibbereen,
Who was terribly haughty and mean,
    When women were nigh,
    He'd unbutton his fly,
And shout, 'Look — 'tis fit for the Queen.'

*   *   *

There was a young lass from Fermoy,
With a shape like a capital, 'I',
    When they said — 'It's too bad,'
    She learned how to pad.
Which shows you that figures can lie !

       *   *   *

Every time an Irish 'County type' swoons,
Her breasts they pop out like balloons.
    But her butler stands by
    With hauteur in his eye,
And puts them back gently with spoons !

       *   *   *

Two lassies who strolled near the Gallarus,
Had eyes that were brighter than phosphorus,
    A Corkman cried : 'Troth !
    I'll marry you both.'
But they laughingly said : 'You must toss for us.'

       *   *   *

A young lass from near Lisbellaw
Was hurt by her low strapless bra,
    She loosened one wire
    Whereupon the entire
Dress fell — Guess what the RUC saw ?

       *   *   *

A farmer from near Castlemaine
Whose legs were cut off by a train.
    When his friends said : 'How sad,'
    He replied : 'I am glad.
For I've lost my varicose vein.'

*   *   *

An Irish lass loves not her lover
So much as she loves his love of her.
    Then loves she her lover
    For love of her lover.
Or love of her love of her lover ?

*   *   *

There was a blackguard from near Croom,
Who lured a poor girl to her doom.
    He not only seduced her,
    But robbed her and goosed her.
And left her to pay for the room.

*   *   *

A young lassie from Dungarvan Bay,
Who never let men have their way,
    But a brawny young spark,
    One night in the park . . . .
Now she goes to the park every day.

*   *   *

There was an old man from The Combe
Who farted and filled a balloon,
      The balloon went so high,
      That it stuck in the sky,
And stank out the Man in the Moon !

* * *

Said a girl making love in a shanty :
'My dear, your legs are all slanty.'
      He replied : 'I can use
      Any angle I choose,
I do as I please — I'm from Bantry !'

* * *

A lassie from near to Stradbally
Who is worried by lovers so many
      That the saucy young elf
      Means to raffle herself,
And the tickets are two for a penny !

* * *

A young man from near Carrighart
Known from Cork to Fair Head for his farts.
      When they asked : 'Why so loud ?'
      He replied with head bowed :
'When I farts, sure I farts from the heart.'

* * *

'Twas an Irish farmer who said :
'Can I take off me leggins in bed?'
   His brother said :'No.
   Wherever you go,
You must wear them until you are dead.'

     *   *   *

A farmer from near Ballineen,
Who grew so abnormally lean.
   And flat and compressed,
   That his back squeezed his chest,
And sideways he couldn't be seen.

     *   *   *

A lass from the City of Cork,
Was shortly expecting the 'stork',
   When the doctor walked in
   With a business-like grin,
A pickaxe, a spade, and a fork.

     *   *   *

A lass from the town of Macroom
Made love to the Man in the Moon.
   'Well, it had been great fun,'
   She remarked when 'twas done —
But I'm sorry to leave him so soon.

     *   *   *

A lassie from near Lake Currane
Had triplets named — Jill, Jack and Sean.
    'Twas fun in the breedin . . .
    But hell in the feedin' —
She hadn't a spare breast for Sean.

*   *   *

A fat woman from near to Lispole,
Had a thought so exceedingly droll.
    She went to the ball,
    Dressed in nothing at all,
And spent the night at the 'Rock and the Roll'

*   *   *

An Irishman owned an ould barge,
But his nose was exceedingly large.
    But in fishing by night
    It supported a light —
Which helped the old man with his charge.

*   *   *

A woman at the Fair of Fermoy,
Had a terrible cast in her eye,
    No person would dare,
    To respond to her stare,
But she never could understand why !

*   *   *

A lassie from near Boherbue,
Who said to her lover : 'You see —
    If you take me, of course,
    You must do it by force —
But God knows you are stronger than me!'

        *   *   *

A young lass on the fair stand of Howe,
Who said that she didn't know how.
    Then an Irishman caught her,
    And bloody soon taught her,
And did it without any row.

        *   *   *

A tourist just near Dunamark,
Who, when he made love had to bark,
    His wife was a bitch,
    With a terrible itch —
So, Glengarriff can't sleep after dark !

        *   *   *

A pretty young lass from Kilquane,
While walking was caught in the rain.
    She ran — almost flew.
    Her complexion did too !
And she reached home exceedingly plain.

        *   *   *

There is a Creator named God,
Whose doings are sometimes quite odd.
  He made Kerrymen cute,
  And Tipperarymen mute,
Which when all's said and done is just cod !

*   *   *

A man from Achill Island said : 'Do
Tell me how I can add two and two ?
  I'm not very sure
  That it doesn't make four —
But I fear that is always too few.'

*   *   *

'Tis strange how some Irishmen honour
A specimen called 'prima donna',
  But they say not a thing,
  Of how she can sing —
But write reams of the clothes she had on her!

*   *   *

And here's to the good old Cape Clear —
Where long after midnight flows beer.
  And the Capers so gay
  Works twelve hours a day
At free grants and free dole they just jeer !

*   *   *

There's a lassie from Castletownbere,
With tresses of lovely dark hair.
    Which I'd love to be feeling,
    And sweet kisses stealing,
And that little bit more — sure I'd dare !

*   *   *

A farmer from Ballymacoda,
Was awarded a special diploma.
    For telling apart,
    A masculine fart —
For a similar female aroma !

*   *   *

A lass from the town of Portnoo
Found love-making effected her hue.
    She presented to sight
    Her face pink, her breasts white —
And another part — red, black and blue.

*   *   *

A man from the town of Rosegreen
Grew daily abnormally lean.
    So flat and compressed —
    That his back touched his chest,
And sideways he couldn't be seen!

*   *   *

An Irish lad treated for hernia,
Said to his surgeon : 'Alleluia'.
   'When slitting my middle,
    Be sure not to fiddle,
With things that do not concern ya!'

*   *   *

An Irish lad trying to hide,
Was once at a funeral spied.
   When asked : 'Who was dead?'
    He wonderingly said :
'I don't know. I just came for the ride!'

*   *   *

A woman who lived outside Cobh,
Got a notion to marry, by Jove,
   She nabbed a young sailor,
    Who swore he'd ne'er fail her.
Which ended his days on the rove !

*   *   *

In Donnybrook dwells a strange race
So far from the Queen — what disgrace !
   But they strive to be merry,
    With pre-dinner sherry —
And they toast her, and roast her, with grace !

*   *   *

How sad for to see Baltimore !
Where the Irish are now to the fore.
God be with the old days
And our dear British ways —
But alas and alack, they're no more !

*   *   *

A visitor to the great Head of Bolus,
Went dancing in Knightstown as Venus.
A priest told her how rude
'Twas to come there quite nude,
Then he got her a leaf from a greenhouse !

*   *   *

A hardy old man from Clonfert,
Was born on the day of his birth.
He was married, they say,
On his wife's wedding day,
And he died when he quitted this earth !

*   *   *

A young lass from near Killenaule
Wore a newspaper dress to a ball.
The dress it caught fire
Burnt up the entire —
Front page, sporting section and all !

*   *   *

A tourist at fair Galway Bay,
Made fireworks on a hot summer's day.
    He dipped his cigar
    In the gunpowder jar,
Now the fish have got fat in the bay !

*   *   *

There was an old lady from Mallow,
Whose complexion was just very sallow,
    When asked for the cause,
    She replied without pause —
'Sure, three times a day I chew tallow!'

*   *   *

Sure, I'm living in Ballydehob,
Away from that damn city mob.
    I go to Confession,
    Attend every Mission,
Say the Rosary each night by the hob !

*   *   *

There was a young lad from Glengarriff,
Who liked to dress up as a Sheriff,
    He toted his guns,
    Swore he'd save all the nuns,
From the guys who looked like Omar Sharif!

*   *   *

A big ship came into Cork Quay,
Full of sailors just mad for a lay !
    The whores of the city,
      Rushed on board without pity,
In their hurry they smashed the gangway.

*   *   *

A young lass from near to Ardkeragh
Whose body had plenty of meat there.
    She said : 'Marry me, fast
      And you'll find that my ass,
Is the spot for to warm your cold feet there.'

*   *   *

An Irishman with a long beard,
Who said : 'It is just as I feared —
    Two Cocks and a Hen
      Four Ducks and a Wren,
Have all built their nests in my beard!'

*   *   *

I'm in love with a lass near Ardfert,
Whose hair is so scant it won't part.
    She's cross-eyed and thin,
      And as ugly as sin.
But then, she has such a good heart !

*   *   *

A young man near the Bridge of Blackwater,
Who daily got shorter and shorter,
    'The reason,' he said.
    'Is the brains in me head,
Get so heavy that I fear a disorder.'

    *   *   *

A fat woman who lived near the Bride,
Her shoelaces once came untied.
    She didn't dare stoop,
    For fear she would poop,
And she cried, and she cried, and she cried !

    *   *   *

There's a sweet little place Courtmacsherry
You can get there by road or by ferry
    Some girls wear no panties
    Or other such scanties
But most have held on to their cherry.

    *   *   *

There's a wood near the fair Castlefreke
Where short-taken gents sometimes leak
    If you've been well brought up
    And are not a pup
Of the strange things you'll see, you'll ne'er speak.

    *   *   *

A baritone who strolled near Falcarragh
Slipped one day on a yellow banana.
     He was shagged for a year
     But once more did appear,
This time as a rousing soprano !

*   *   *

A lass a few miles from Kilkee
Chatted up every man she could see.
     When it came to a test
     She was reckoned the best
And practice makes perfect, you see.

*   *   *

A lassie from near Dromahilly,
Had a craving to walk Piccadilly,
     She said : 'Ain't it funny ?
     It ain't for the money !
But if I don't take it it's silly.'

*   *   *

A lass on the island of Clear
Once knelt in the moonlight all bare,
     She prayed to her God,
     For a bit on the sod,
And a hippy boy answered her prayer !

*   *   *

In the village that's well known as Leap
The girls there would sure give one pep
    They've a wonderful carriage
    And are red-ripe for marriage
Don't go further if you're taking that step.

*   *   *

Near the sea by the famed Inchydoney
Some sights you will see there are funny
    The lovers together
    Bobbing up in the heather
And the clergy play cards for the money.

*   *   *

In the crags near the wild Mizen Head
Sure the couples you'd swear they were wed
    They lose all their shame
    And forget their good name
For they think that the grass is the bed.

*   *   *

Oh I'd love to live near Adrigole
And draw fifty a week on the dole
    And to hear the birds sing
    And the waterfalls ring
And a big cosy fire of free coal.

*   *   *

In the Gaeltacht of sweet Ballingearry
Where the Gaels of both sexes are airy
    If you want to make love
    It's O.K. from Above
If you do it through Irish — and be wary !

*   *   *

Oh I love to stop off in Millstreet
And sample the poteen so neat
    For despite the poor guards
    It's made in backyards
While they walk in the cold on the beat.

*   *   *

I'm saying me prayers to St. Jude
To keep away thoughts that are lewd
    He'll do what he can
    To get me a man
And we'll wed, and we'll bed, is that rude ?

*   *   *

To the gay town of old Skibbereen,
Came a tinker abnormally lean,
    They fed him so well,
    That he started to swell,
And by Christmas he looked like a Dean.

*   *   *

SLAN LEAT

I hope that these Limericks did please you
And some more, I trust, did just tease you
    I hope you did laugh
    At the odd funny gaff
For they're written to relax and to ease you.